BOOKS
THAT HAVE SHAPED
THE WORLD

....

Books
THAT HAVE SHAPED
The World

By
Fred Eastman

Professor of Biography, Literature and Drama
Chicago Theological Seminary

CHICAGO
American Library Association
1937

....

PUBLISHED JUNE 1937
SECOND PRINTING MAY 1938

....

TO THE READER

YOU have stood bewildered in a great library? The bewilderment was natural. Surrounded by tens of thousands of books, you didn't know which to choose. The wrong ones would waste your time. The right ones—which were they? Ralph Waldo Emerson in his essay, "Books," says, "In this lottery there are at least fifty to a hundred blanks to a prize. It seems then as if some charitable soul, after losing a great deal of time among the false books and alighting upon a few true ones. . . would do a right act in naming those which have been bridges or ships to carry him safely over dark morasses and barren oceans, into the heart of sacred cities, into palaces and temples. This would be best done by those great masters of books who from time to time appear . . . whose eyes sweep the whole horizon of learning. But private readers, reading purely for love of the book, would serve us by leaving each the shortest note of what he found."

As a private reader, "reading purely for the love of the book," I have compiled these lists in biography, drama, and other literature. Yet that cold statement fails to express the joy I have experienced in assembling them or my eagerness to share them with you, the prospective reader. These books are not paper and ink and cloth; they are persons. For the most part they are a company of immortals who have weathered the centuries and are now marching toward eternity. They invited me to walk with them a little way. They opened their hearts to me. They told me of their adventures, their romances, their meditations and their explorations of the inner world. They lifted my horizons. They made me laugh and cry and rejoice to be living in the same world. . . . They invite you, too.

Of course the two hundred books recommended here are not the only great or significant ones. They are foundational and important, but hundreds of others are waiting to delight you. Your librarian will introduce you to them if you will give her half a chance.

F. E.

Chicago, 1937

CONTENTS

WALKING WITH THE GREAT

WHY read biographies? For the fun of it! It's fun to discover young Lincoln Steffens exhibiting his horse-training skill by having his sisters and their girl friends lie prone upon the ground while he puts his pony through his paces stepping over them. When his father punishes him, it's fun to hear him blubber, "They were only girls!"

It's fun to turn a page and see young Charles Darwin eagerly holding one rare beetle in his right fist, another in his left, and then suddenly catching sight of a third which he simply must have for his collection. What to do? In a flash he puts one of the beetles in his mouth and reaches for the third. But the mouth-imprisoned beetle doesn't care for this procedure and squirts its acid down Charles's throat so that in a fit of coughing he loses all three little beasts.

It's fun to turn another page and come across young Michael Pupin standing before an immigration official and declaring that he has three friends in America. "What friends?" inquires the official. "Benjamin Franklin, Abraham Lincoln, and Harriet Beecher Stowe," replies the lad stoutly. It's fun to see him making his way up from the landing at Battery park, his last nickel spent for a prune-pie that was all pits, and running afoul of a bunch of toughs who knock his fez from his head. It's fun to see him sail into them and lick them one by one.

It's fun to see Ralph Waldo Emerson and his son trying to get a rebellious calf into a barn. Ralph Waldo pushes and his son pulls, but the calf stubbornly stiffens its legs and budges not. Father and son exchange positions; but still no movement of the calf. Along comes an Irish serving maid, giggles at their dilemma, then puts a maternal finger into the calf's mouth and leads it gently to the barn. That night Emerson writes in his journal, "I like people who can *do* things!"

But it's more than the fun of anecdote and incident. It's the fun of the chase. You start out to discover that illusive thing, a man's personality; not the outer facts about his life, when he was born, where he went to school, what titles he won, but the inner man, the soul that hides behind the facts. It eludes you and you keep after it. It slips a date or an office or a book before your eyes and says, "See what I did!" But you reply, "I'm not so much interested in what you did, but *why* you wanted to do it. You had *power;* where did you get it?" No life yields an easy answer to that question. If you find it you'll know you've been in a chase.

That's only one of the joys of reading biographies. Here's another: to make new friends. You may not be able to make friends with the man next door and he may not be worthy of your friendship. In all the turbulent city in which you live you may know of no one with whom you can commune. But go down to the book shop or the public library. Ask for Paul Sabatier's *Life of St. Francis of Assisi* and in two evenings' time you will be walking shoulder to shoulder with one of the humblest and quaintest and most inspiring souls of all human history. Or ask for Francis Hirst's *Life of Thomas Jefferson* and in another week you will be going around an inch taller as you try to keep the stride of that giant. George Gordon, in his autobiography, records his discovery of the value of such reading: "It gives one a place in the best society of the world. . . . This association with the greatest minds of the world, or with a selection of them, is on the intellectual side what we mean by the communion of the saints."

It is no fanciful thing—this finding friends among the shades. Nothing could be more real. Albert Schweitzer never met Goethe in the flesh. Yet he says that in his experience he met him seven times. First, it was in the field of philosophy when he had to choose between a speculative philosophy and an insignificant and well-nigh abandoned nature philosophy. He chose the latter and found to his amazement and joy that Goethe more than a century earlier had made the same choice. A second time he met him in student days when he read of Goethe setting out in a November rain to visit a minister's son who was in the midst of spiritual difficulties. Schweitzer himself had wanted to devote his time to his studies and not be bothered by the human needs of his fellows, but when he read that incident of the great Goethe it came over him that if Goethe could take the time, surely he could. And he did.

Again, Schweitzer found in his experience that intellectual work went better when practical work went side-by-side with it and so he disciplined himself to keep the two always balanced, only to find that Goethe had been through the same discipline. When Schweitzer felt a call to leave his philosophical work and his music to take up medical missionary work in Africa it meant that he must put in long years in medical school. "But," in his own words, "I was able to reflect that Goethe too had left intellectual work to return to the natural sciences." (Will professors of the natural sciences please note!)

There came a time in the African forest when Schweitzer's hospital was endangered by famine. To provide food it was necessary to make a clearing in the forest and start a small plantation. But the native workers would bow to no authority but that of the "old doctor" as they called Schweitzer, who was not yet forty. So for weeks and months he stood in the forest worrying over refractory laborers in order to help them perform the simplest tasks of cutting down trees and pulling roots and planting seed. "Whenever I got reduced to despair," he says, "I thought how Goethe had devised for the final activities of his Faust the task of winning from the sea land on which men could live and feed themselves. And thus Goethe stood at my side in the swampy forest as my smiling comforter, and the man who really understood."

And here's another joy: to see how others have faced the struggles that we face. The great experiences of life are common to us all—birth, love, adventure, depression, defeat, success, death. But human beings do not react in the same way to their common experiences. To see how others, and especially the great, have faced these experiences and mastered them, or compromised with them, helps us to follow or avoid their example.

That sounds pious. But it isn't. Take, for instance, the perplexing business of bringing up children. Every parent wants his child to have a good home. But what is a good home? Not necessarily a rich home, nor a poor one, but one that will develop the children best. You can study the abstract principles in books on child training. But open a biography, such as John Ruskin's *Praeterita*, and you have at once an unforgettable picture. There before you and in action are some of the factors that produced a man of power. And after the picture comes his own comment upon those factors. Here is a part of it:

I had been taught the perfect meaning of *peace*, in thought, act, and word.

I never had heard my father's or mother's voice once raised in any question with each other; nor seen an angry, or even slightly hurt or offended glance in the eyes of either. I had never heard a servant scolded. . . . I had never seen a moment's trouble or disorder in any household matter; nor anything whatever done in a hurry. . . . I had no conception of such a feeling as anxiety. . . . I had never done any wrong that I knew of—beyond occasionally delaying the commitment to heart of some improving sentence, that I might watch a wasp upon the window pane, or a bird in the cherry tree; and I had never seen any grief.

Next to this quite priceless gift of peace, I had received the perfect understanding of the natures of *obedience* and *faith*. I obeyed word, or lifted finger, of father or mother, simply as a ship her helm; not only without idea of resistance, but receiving the direction as a part of my own life and force. . . . And my practice in faith was soon complete; nothing was ever promised me that was not given; nothing ever threatened me that was not inflicted, and nothing ever told me that was not true. . . .

There is the record of a laboratory experiment. Compare that home with young Byron's. See Byron's emotionally unstable mother flying into a fit of rage, chasing the lad around the room and calling him a "lame brat." And without abstract discussions about the educational elements that enter into the making of a home you know why Ruskin developed the "most analytical mind in Europe" and why Byron grew up with such undisciplined passions in his own frame that they wellnigh wrecked his body so that he sang at the age of thirty-six:

> My days are in the yellow leaf,
>   The flowers and fruits of love are gone,
> The worm, the canker, and the grief
>   Are mine alone.

[14]

Or take the common experience of trying to face life with a handicap. What is it—deafness, blindness, paralysis, poverty, stuttering? In biographies you shall find comfort. Yes, and shame for self-pity. Deafness? Beethoven began to go deaf when he was thirty years of age and composed his ninth symphony after he was so deaf that he never heard a note of it. Thomas Edison was so deaf that the only way he could hear a phonograph record of his own invention was by biting his teeth in the edge of the cabinet and getting the vibrations through the bones of his skull. Edward S. Martin, dean of American essayists and loved wherever ripe wisdom and gentle humor are loved, was deaf for more than twenty years.

Blindness? Professor Frost, head of the great Yerkes observatory, for a quarter of a century gave to the world the news about the stars and the doings along the Milky Way. But he was blind and did not see the heavens he loved so well. He figured them out by mathematics. Milton's best writings came after he became blind. Weak eyes? Samuel Johnson had them, but somehow managed to compile the first really great dictionary in the English language.

Ill-health? Darwin had forty years of it while he worked upon the scientific hypotheses that have changed the thinking of the whole world. Emerson had it, and weak eyes as well, but he left a collection of essays and poetry in the front rank of American literature. Charles Dickens had it, but he gave to the world the healthiest collection of characters in fiction. Queen Elizabeth had a high batting average among the queens, but she has been described in books upon her medical record as suffering from syphilis, eye-strain, fits, "achy" teeth, smallpox, stomach disorders, ulcers, dropsy, rheumatism and gout, not to mention occasional complete breakdowns! Michelangelo had a violent intestinal disorder, Molière had weak lungs, Ibsen had diabetes, Loyola had a leg smashed by a cannon ball and went through two serious amputations without anesthetic; Handel had one hand paralyzed, Rubens had gout and neuralgia. It is no wonder that a consideration of some of the most beloved artists leads George Jean Nathan to declare, "Art is the child of ill-health." Disraeli, George Fox, John Burroughs, Francis Asbury, Thomas Carlyle, Voltaire, and Schleiermacher all had ill health, but their work went on notwithstanding.

Poverty? The list of the financially handicapped among the great is so long that one wonders if the first step toward permanent achievement might be securing release from all bondage to property and things. Certainly St. Francis demonstrated for himself, his followers, and the rest of the world that joy and peace might be found by divorcing oneself from all material possessions. Charles Lamb supported himself by a clerkship while he wrote the essays that kept a smile on England's face. Matthew Arnold, in order to practice and preach the power of culture to save civilization from anarchy and in order to write the poetry and the critical essays that have enriched our classics, earned his daily bread as an inspector of secondary schools—a task whose drudgery must have galled his sensitive spirit. Name your handicap—whatever it is you have but to open the door of biographies to find others with the same symptoms.

Or is it the opposition of your fellow men, rather than physical and economic handicaps, that troubles you? Put your eye to the keyhole of biographies and see others facing the same opposition and worse. Watch St. Teresa in her crusade to purify life in the monasteries meeting the opposition of a wealthy and corrupt clergy. See Francis of Assisi haled to court by his own father and disowned. Look at Savonarola carrying on single handed a battle against the powerful Lorenzo de Medici and his allies. Behold Joan cast to the flames. Or in more modern times observe the scientists pouncing upon Darwin, the literary critics upon Browning and Wordsworth, and the politicians upon Lincoln, Woodrow Wilson, Hoover and Roosevelt. And you turn away from the keyhole thanking God that you have a splinter in your thumb instead of a spear in your side.

Greatest of all the joys in reading biographies is the joy of discovering courage—courage in action. Courage facing handicaps. Courage bucking the opposition. Courage venturing across unknown seas with Columbus, or into the icy wastes with

Peary, or through the jungles with Livingstone, or down into the pit of toryism with Kier Hardie, or out upon the social frontiers with Jane Addams and Graham Taylor. Here is Beecher howled at and assaulted by an angry mob in London as he tries to win sympathy for the cause of freeing American slaves.

And here is Captain Scott of the Antarctic, feet frozen, food exhausted, lying down in his tent to die, writing in a quavering hand to Barrie wishing he might hear the "songs and cheery conversation" of his hard bitten companions, and then penning at the conclusion of his diary that last heartrending appeal to the public, "For God's sake, take care of our people!" Courage—to forget self and think of others!

* * *

Two questions naturally arise in the mind of anyone who has decided to explore further the joys of reading biographies: How go about it to get the most out of it? and What lives are most worth exploring?

Here is a method which may be found useful in answer to the first question: Take fourteen cards, or small sheets of paper, when beginning to read a biography. At the top of each write one of the following subheads and then as you read classify your notes accordingly, putting down under each subhead the data most worth remembering.

[18]

1. *Heredity.* Father, mother, and other forebears.
2. *Early environment.* The nation and times. Home and local community. School. Church. Personalities.
3. *Later environment.* Home and family. Friends. Other elements.
4. *Purpose.* Note the various purposes by which the character steered his life's activities. Did he come finally to center his efforts around a single purpose? What was it?
5. *Opposition.* Who or what opposed him and why?
6. *Handicaps.* Physical, social, and economic.
7. *What did he do?* His most notable achievements.
8. *What did he say?* Characteristic utterances.
9. *Dramatic or vivid scenes of his life.*
10. *Religious beliefs or convictions.*
11. *Failures.* Vocational and personal.
12. *Personality.* Dominant moods and attitudes.
13. *Sources of his power.* Your own judgment as to the relative importance of such sources as heredity, physical endowment, home influences, friends, religious convictions, prayer and meditation, singleness of purpose, hard work, self-discipline, knowledge, freedom from financial cares, supernormal experiences such as visions, trances, and the like, other factors.
14. *Bibliography.*

I would hardly be bold enough to suggest the above outline for use beyond my own classes in biographies except for this fact: I submitted it to the late Gamaliel Bradford, dean of American biographers, and I shall always prize the letter he wrote in comment upon it and upon the syllabus which I shall include below. He said:

. . . I am exceedingly interested in the questions in your Outline, for it is just precisely on that line that I have been doing my own biographical work for the last twenty years. . . . Your syllabus is admirably selected and I should not feel disposed to criticize it, if I were competent to do so. . . .

The advantage of such an outline is not only that it helps in preserving one's notes, but it frees one in part at least from the prejudices and biases of the biographer. It helps separate the facts from the opinions. Until recently few biographers seemed to think it necessary or desirable to keep their own opinions and biases in the background. Moreover, when you have accumulated half a dozen such outlines from the reading of as many lives you have the fun of comparing them—their respective heredities, home influences, loves, purposes, and religions.

As for the lives most worth exploring, two lists are appended: The first is a classified one of great lives from the 12th to the 20th centuries. Around nearly every one of these lives many biographies have been written. Bibliographies may be found at the end of the articles concerning each of them in any good encyclopedia. Some of the books are long, others short, some easy, others difficult. Your local librarian will help you select the ones most suited to your particular needs. The second list is of about fifty significant biographies.

A Classified List of Great Lives

Religious Leaders and Social Reformers	Statesmen	Scientists	Artists, Writers, Philosophers
1100			
Hildebrand, 1015–85			
Anselm, 1033–1109			
St. Bernard, 1091–1153			
Becket, Th. a', 1119–70	Saladin, 1137–93		Abelard, 1079–1142
Innocent III, 1161–1216	Langton, S., 1150 (?)–1228		
St. Dominic, 1170–1221			
St. Francis, 1182–1226			
1200			
Aquinas, Th.,, (?)1227–74 (?)	Louis IX, 1216–70		Bacon, R., 1214–94
			Dante, 1265–1321
			Duns Scotus, 1265–1308
			Giotto di Bondone, 1266–1337
Wm. of Occam, 1270–1349			Marsilio of Padua, 1270–1343
1300			
			Petrarch, 1304–74
			Boccacio, 1313–75
Wyclif, 1324–84			Chaucer, 1328–1400
			Froissart, 1337–1410
Huss, 1369–1415			Kempis, Th. a', 1380–1471
			Fra Angelico, 1387–1455

[21]

A CLASSIFIED LIST OF GREAT LIVES—*Cont'd*

Religious Leaders and Social Reformers	Statesmen	Scientists	Artists, Writers, Philosophers
		1400	
Jeanne d'Arc, 1412–31	Machiavelli, 1469–1527	Columbus, Christopher, 1446–1506	Caxton, 1422–91
Savonarola, 1452–98	Wolsey, 1471–1530	Copernicus, 1473–1543	DaVinci, 1452–1519
Luther, 1483–1546	More, T., 1478–1535		Erasmus, 1466–1536
Zwingli, 1484–1531	Hutton, Ulrich v., 1488–1523		Michelangelo, 1475–1564
Cranmer, 1489–1556	Henry VIII, 1491–1547		Raphael, 1483–1520
Loyola, 1491–1556			
		1500	
Xavier, 1506–52			Tyndale, (??)–1536
Calvin, 1509–64			Cellini, 1500–71
Knox, J., 1513–72	William Silent, 1533–84		
St. Teresa, 1515–82	Elizabeth, Queen, 1533–1603		
Cartwright, Th., 1534–1603	Raleigh, Sir W., 1552–1618	Galileo, 1564–1642	Bacon, 1561–1626
Francis de Sales, 1567–1622	Eliot, Sir Jn., 1592–1632	Kepler, (?)1571–1630	Marlowe, 1564–93
Robinson, Jn., 1575–1625	Gustavus Adolphus, 1594–1632		Shakespeare, 1564–1616
Ussher, 1581–1656	Cromwell, 1599–1658	Descartes, 1596–1650	Rubens, 1577–1640
Hutchinson, Ann, 1590–1643			Hobbes, 1588–1679
			Van Dyck, 1599–1641

A CLASSIFIED LIST OF GREAT LIVES—Cont'd

1600

Religious Leaders and Social Reformers	Statesmen	Scientists	Artists, Writers, Philosophers
Eliot, Jn., 1604–90			Rembrandt, 1606–69
Williams, Roger, 1604–83			Milton, 1608–74
Fox, Geo., 1624–91			Bossuet, 1627–1704
Bunyan, J., 1628–88		Pascal, 1623–62	Dryden, 1631–1700
Marquette, J., 1637–75	Louis XIV (France), 1638–1715		Locke, 1632–1704
Mather, Increase, 1638–1723	Penn, William, 1644–1718		Spinoza, 1632–77
Baxter, R., 1651–91	Marlborough, Duke, 1650–1722	Newton, I., 1642–1727	Wren, C., 1632–1723
Fenelon, 1651–1715	Walpole, 1676–1745	Leibnitz, 1646–1716	Rousseau, J. B., 1670–1741
Mather, C., 1663–1728			Handel, 1684–1759
Swedenborg, 1688–1772			Bach, 1685–1750
			Voltaire, 1694–1778

1700

Religious Leaders and Social Reformers	Statesmen	Scientists	Artists, Writers, Philosophers
Wesley, J., 1703–91	Franklin, 1706–90		Johnson, S., 1709–84
Edwards, Jonathan, 1703–58	Frederick II (the Great), 1712–86		
Wesley, C., 1707–88	Blackstone, 1723–80		Hume, 1711–76
Whitefield, Geo., 1714–70	Clive, R., 1725–74		Rousseau, J. J., 1712–78
Brainerd, D., 1718–47	Burke, Ed., 1729–97		Diderot, 1713–84
Woolman, Jn., 1720–72	Catherine the Great, 1729–96	Herschel, Sir Wm., 1738–1822	Reynolds, Sir J., 1723–92
	Washington, W., 1732–99		Kant, 1724–1804
	Hastings, W., 1732–1818		Goldsmith, 1728–74

A CLASSIFIED LIST OF GREAT LIVES—*Cont'd*

Religious Leaders and Social Reformers	Statesmen	Scientists	Artists, Writers, Philosophers
		1700 (cont'd)	
Raikes, Robert, 1735–1811 Asbury, Francis, 1745–1816	Jefferson, 1743–1826 Mirabeau, 1749–91 Madison, J., 1751–1836 Marshall, J., 1755–1835	Lamarck, 1744–1829 Laplace, 1749–1827	Paine, Thos., 1737–1809 Goethe, 1749–1832
		1750	
	Lafayette, 1757–1834 Hamilton, Alex., 1757–1804 Nelson, Adm., 1758–1805 Monroe, J., 1758–1831 Pitt, Wm., 1759–1806 Robespierre, 1759–94 Wilberforce, 1759–1833 Napoleon, 1769–1821 Wellington, Duke, 1769–1852 Metternich, 1773–1859	Audubon, 1780–1851 Stephenson, Geo., 1781–1848 Faraday, 1791–1867 Herschel, J. F. W., 1792–1871	Maimon, 1754–1800 Mozart, 1756–91 Burns, R., 1759–96 Schiller, 1759–1805 Beethoven, 1770–1827 Hegel, 1770–1831 Wordsworth, Wm., 1770–1850 Scott, Walter, 1771–1832 Lamb, 1775–1834 Landor, W. S., 1775–1864 Byron, 1788–1824 Schopenhauer, 1788–1860 Shelley, 1792–1822 Arnold, Th., 1795–1842 Carlyle, 1795–1881
Carey, Wm., 1761–1834 Schleiermacher, 1768–1834 Owen, R., 1771–1858 Cartwright, P., 1785–1872 Judson, Ad., 1788–1850			

A CLASSIFIED LIST OF GREAT LIVES—*Cont'd*

1800

Religious Leaders and Social Reformers	Statesmen	Scientists	Artists, Writers, Philosophers
Newman, J. H., 1801–90			Macaulay, 1800–59
Young, Brigham, 1801–77			Hugo, V., 1802–85
Bushnell, 1802–76			Emerson, 1803–82
	Cobden, 1804–65		Sterling, J., 1806–44
	Disraeli, 1804–81		Mill, J. S., 1806–73
	Garibaldi, 1807–82		Mendelssohn, 1809–47
	Lincoln, 1809–65	Darwin, 1809–82	Tennyson, 1809–92
	Gladstone, 1809–98		Liszt, 1811–66
	Cavour, 1810–61		Dickens, 1812–70
			Browning, 1812–89
Livingstone, D., 1813–73			Bronte, C., 1816–55
Beecher, H. W., 1813–87	Bismarck, 1815–98		Marx, K., 1818–83
			Kingsley, 1819–75
			Eliot, Geo., 1819–80
			Whitman, 1819–92
			Ruskin, 1819–1900
			Spencer, 1820–1903
			Nightingale, F., 1820–1910
Eddy, Mary B., 1821–1910		Mendel, 1822–84	Arnold, Mat., 1822–88
		Pasteur, 1822–84	Dostoevsky, 1822–81
Bliss, Daniel, 1823–1916		Fabre, J. H., 1823–1915	Renan, E., 1823–92
		Huxley, 1825–95	Ibsen, 1828–1906

A CLASSIFIED LIST OF GREAT LIVES—*Cont'd*

Religious Leaders and Social Reformers	Statesmen	Scientists	Artists, Writers, Philosophers
		1800 (cont'd)	
Booth, Gen. Wm., 1829–1912		Maxwell, J. C., 1831–79	Tolstoy, 1828–1910
Brooks, Ph., 1835–93		Burroughs, Jn., 1837–1921	Ingersoll, 1833–99
			Twain, M., 1835–1910
Abbott, Lyman, 1835–1922	Adams, Henry B., 1838–1918		Morley, Jn., 1838–1923
Gladden, Wash., 1835–1918			Tschaikowsky, 1840–93
		Edison, 1847–1931	Hardy, 1840–1928
Moody, 1837–99		Trudeau, 1848–	James, William, 1842–1910
White, Alex., 1837–1921	Churchill, Lord, 1849–95	Burbank, 1849–1926	Jeffries, R., 1848–87
		1850	
Taylor, Graham, 1851–	Gompers, Samuel, 1850–1924	Osler, Wm., 1849–1919	Stevenson, R. L., 1850–94
	Rhodes, C., 1853–1902	Lodge, Sir O. J., 1851–	Drummond, H., 1851–97
Washington, Bk. T., 1855–1915	Wilson, W., 1856–1924	Freud, S., 1856–	Palmer, Alice F., 1855–95
Addams, Jane, 1860–1935	Roosevelt, T., 1858–1919	Pupin, 1858–1935	Barrie, J. M., 1860–
Rauschenbusch, 1861–1918	Baldwin, Wm. H., 1863–1905	Curie, Marie, 1867–1934, and Pierre, 1859–1906	Bok, E., 1863–1929
	MacDonald, J. R., 1866–	Dewey, John, 1859–	Galsworthy, J., 1867–1933
Jowett, 1864–1923	Lenin, 1870–1924	Marconi, 1874–	Keller, Helen, 1880–
Steiner, Ed. A., 1866–	Mussolini, 1883–	Jung, Carl, 1875–	Mansfield, K., 1890–1923
Rasputin, 1871–1916	Hitler, A., 1889–	Einstein, Albert, 1879	

AN INTRODUCTORY LIST OF BIOGRAPHIES

(Those marked * are available in editions priced at $1 or less.)

---

*ADAMS, Henry, *The Education of.* (Modern Library)

*ADDAMS, Jane. *Twenty Years at Hull House.* (Macmillan)

*AUDUBON, John J., *Life and Adventures,* by Robert Buchanan. (Everyman)

BACH, Johann Sebastian, *Life of,* by Albert Schweitzer. (2 vols.) (Breitkopf & Hartel)

*BURNS, Robert, *Life of,* by J. Lockhart. (Everyman)

BURROUGHS, John, *Life and Letters of,* by Clara Barrus. (Houghton)

*CELLINI, Benvenuto, *Autobiography of.* (Everyman)

CROMWELL, Oliver, *Life of,* by John Morley, (Macmillan)

DARWIN, Charles R., *Life and Letters of,* by Francis Darwin. (2 vols.) (Appleton-Century)

DAVID, *Story of.* I and II Samuel. (The Bible)

DICKINSON, Emily, *Life and Letters of,* by Martha Dickinson Bianchi. (Houghton)

DOSTOEVSKY: *The Man and His Work,* by J. Meier-Graefe. (Harcourt)

EDWARDS, Jonathan, by Arthur Cushman McGiffert, Jr. (Harper)

ELIOT, Charles W., by Henry James. (2 vols.) (Houghton)

EMERSON, Ralph Waldo, *Life of,* by van Wyck Brooks. (Dutton)

[27]

FOX, George, *Seeker and Friend*, by Rufus Jones. (Harper)

*FRANKLIN, Benjamin, *Autobiography of*. (Everyman)

*GLADSTONE, William E., *Life of*, by G. Russell. (Everyman)

*GOETHE, J. Wolfgang, by Emil Ludwig. (Blue Ribbon)

*GOSSE: *Father and Son*, by Edmund Gosse. (Oxford)

HARDY, Thomas, *Life of*, by Florence E. Hardy. (2 vols.) (Macmillan)

HEISER, Victor. *An American Doctor's Odyssey*. (Norton)

HUXLEY, Thomas Henry, *Life and Letters of*, by L. Huxley. (Macmillan)

JEFFERSON, Thomas, *Life and Letters of*, by Francis Hirst. (Macmillan)

*JOHNSON, Samuel, *Life of*, by James Boswell. (Modern Library)

JUDSON, Adoniram. *Splendor of God*, by Honore W. Morrow. (Wm. Morrow)

*KELLER, Helen, *Autobiography of*. (Grosset & Dunlap)

KINGSLEY, Charles, *Letters and Memoirs of*, by Mrs. Kingsley. (Macmillan)

LINCOLN, Abraham, by William E. Barton. (Bobbs-Merrill)

*LINCOLN, Abraham, *The Prairie Years*, by Carl Sandburg. (Blue Ribbon)

LUTHER, Martin, by Arthur Cushman McGiffert. (Appleton-Century)

President MASARYK Tells His Story, by Karel Capek. (Putnam)

[28]

MICHELANGELO, *Life of,* by Romain Rolland. (Duffield)

MOODY, Dwight L., *A Worker in Souls,* by Gamaliel Bradford. (Doran)

OGILVY, Margaret, by her son, J. M. Barrie. (Scribner)

*PASTEUR, Louis, *The Life of,* by R. Vallery-Radot. (Garden City Pub.)

*PLUTARCH'S *Lives.* (Modern Library)

*PUPIN, Michael. *From Immigrant to Inventor,* An Autobiography. (Scribner)

RUSKIN, John. *Praeterita,* An Autobiography. (Page)

SCUDDER, Vida. *On Journey.* (Dutton)

*ST. AUGUSTINE. *Confessions.* (Everyman)

ST. FRANCIS *of Assisi, Life of,* by Paul Sabatier. (Scribner)

STEFFENS, Lincoln, *Autobiography of.* (Harcourt)

STEVENSON, R. L., *An Intimate Portrait of,* by Lloyd Osbourne. (Scribner)

*TOLSTOY, Count Leo, *Life of,* by Aylmer Maude. (2 vols.) (Oxford)

TRUDEAU, E. L. *An Autobiography.* (Doubleday)

*VICTORIA, Queen, by Lytton Strachey. (Blue Ribbon)

*WASHINGTON, Booker T. *Up from Slavery,* An Autobiography. (Burt)

WASHINGTON, George, *Life of,* by Rupert Hughes. (Morrow)

*WESLEY, John. *The Lord's Horseman,* by Umphrey Lee. (Appleton-Century)

WILSON, Woodrow, by R. S. Baker. (4 vols.) (Doubleday)

WELLS, H. G. *Experiment in Autobiography.* (Macmillan)

[29]

WHAT'S IN THE CLASSICS?

H OW do you spend the long winters around here—in reading?" inquired the summer visitor of the Maine coast native. "No," replied the native as he whittled a stick. "Reading is bad. Too much reading rots the mind."

Too much reading of trash probably does rot the mind—assuming the reader of such stuff has a mind to rot. But there are books that build up the mind, books that refresh the spirit by the entertainment, the laughter, the excitement they bring, and other books that develop the inner power by broadening culture and deepening understanding. "Go with mean people," said Emerson, "and you think life is mean. Then read Plutarch and the world is a proud place, peopled with men of positive quality, with heroes and demigods standing around us. . . . If our times be sterile in genius, we must cheer us with books of rich and believing men who had atmosphere and amplitude about them." Books of this sort gradually sift themselves out from the other books of their day. When a book manages to survive this sifting process not only for a year but for decades and centuries, we call it a classic.

There is a notion abroad these days that the classics are highbrow books and only the learned read them. Nothing could be further from the truth as every librarian knows. Recently Mr. Charles H. Compton of the St. Louis Public Library, being fond of certain authors, was curious to find out how many other people were also fond of them, and what kind of people they were. So he looked up the library cards of persons who drew out these books, wrote letters to them, and made some interesting discoveries which he has recorded in his book, *Who Reads What?* He found, for example, that among the readers of Thomas Hardy were ninety-one stenographers, six automobile mechanics and salesmen, two cooks, five Negro maids, three Pullman porters, and the wives of two porters. The readers of Euripides included a drugstore clerk, a statistician, several teachers, a steam fitter, an adjustor, an inspector, a beauty specialist, a butcher, the wife of a brakeman, two bookkeepers, two architects, a clerk, a telephone operator, two accountants, a doctor's wife, a news writer, a piano teacher, and the wife of a manufacturer of labels. Are these highbrows? Hardly. They are simply everyday people who have developed discrimination in their reading.

How does one develop discrimination? There are no rules, of course. But there may be a few guideposts. The wise Emerson put up three of them. "(1) Never read any book," he said, "that is not a year old. (2) Never read any but famed books.

(3) Never read any but what you like. Or, in Shakespeare's phrase:

'No profit comes where no pleasure is ta'en;
In brief, sir, study what you most affect.' "

That third guidepost is a cheerful one. Read only what you most enjoy! Shun all books that you would read only out of a sense of duty. Books should be like guests in our homes, invited because we want to laugh with them and swap yarns with them, not because we *ought* to have them. To be sure there are some books which we must have because of the information, the cold facts, they contain—encyclopedias, geographies, guide and cookbooks, scientific treatises and professional manuals—but let's treat them as we treat the men who bring the necessary coal to our cellars: pay them, give them a cup of coffee in the kitchen, and ask them to make as little noise as possible. Let us keep the front of our houses and the front of our heads for the books we invite as welcome guests because we expect to enjoy them.

This does not mean that the enjoyment of a book always lies on the surface or that the first page starts you off with a thrill. The richest kernels are often covered by a hard shell. The novels of Dickens, Scott, and Hardy usually have lengthy, if not tiresome, introductions. You have to sit quietly for a while with Charles Lamb before you see his eyes begin to twinkle and the smile play around his mouth. You must think yourself back into the temple of Dionysus in the midst of some twenty thousand Greeks of the fifth century B.C. before you can get the most out of Agamemnon or Oedipus or Electra.

This brings us to the larger question, "What does literature do for one beyond giving enjoyment?" The best answer I have ever seen to that question is one made by C. Alphonso Smith in a little book[1] first published more than twenty years ago. This in substance was his answer:

It can express your emotions.
It can keep before you the vision of the ideal.
It can give you a better knowledge of human nature.
It can restore the past to you.
It can help you see the glory of the commonplace.

When any book or series of books does that for you, it has made you a bigger person.

How does literature do these things? How, first, does it express your emotions? It expresses your emotions by describing your own experiences and your inner reactions to them. As a child you probably climbed a cherry tree. Does the experience come back to you in these lines from Robert Louis Stevenson's "Foreign Lands"[2]:

> Up into the cherry tree
> Who should climb but little me?
> I held the trunk with both my hands
> And looked abroad on foreign lands.

---

[1]*What Can Literature Do for Me?* (Doubleday, Doran)
[2]From *A Child's Garden of Verses.* (Scribner)

[33]

I saw the next door garden lie,
    Adorned with flowers, before my eye,
And many pleasant places more
    That I had never seen before.

I saw the dimpling river pass
    And be the sky's blue looking-glass;
The dusty roads go up and down
    With people tramping in to town.

If I could find a higher tree,
    Farther and farther I should see,
To where the grown-up river slips
    Into the sea among the ships;

To where the roads on either hand
    Lead onward into fairy land,
Where all the children dine at five,
    And all the playthings come alive.

Also as a child you rebelled against rice pudding, or was it spinach? Milne brings back that rebellion and expresses it for you with a chuckle in his verses beginning:

What is the matter with Mary Jane?
    She's crying with all her might and main,
And she won't eat her dinner—rice pudding again—
    What *is* the matter with Mary Jane?

As you grew older you had a case of puppy love. Your adolescent awkwardness and your limited power of expression made ludicrous your attempts to communicate to your beloved the divine passion within you. Zona Gale has caught you and photographed you in the story of Peter, the inarticulate young lover in her one-act play, *The Neighbours*.[3]

PETER: Mis' Abel! Why don't she treat me right?

MIS' ABEL: Treat *you* right? (PETER, *his momentary courage going, takes the chair on over to the cupboard, turns, nods mutely.*) Why, I don't see how she can. Near as I can make out, you never open your head when you're with her.

PETER: (*Climbing on chair.*) It's funny about me, Mis' Abel. (*From the chair.*) Honest, I dunno what to do about me, sometimes.

MIS' ABEL: Well, *stop* thinkin' about you so much.

PETER: (*Spreading out his hands.*) I do try to. But when I try to think how to stop myself thinking about myself, there's myself thinkin' about me.

MIS' ABEL: Think about somethin' else, then! Get me down that basket. You can stand and talk to me all day. I don't see why you can't talk to her.

PETER: (*Reaching for basket.*) I could talk all right enough. But my tongue won't. I could—but my tongue, it won't. (*Turns with the basket.*) Why, some girls I know I can jolly like the dickens. But Inez—when she comes along, Mis' Abel, I can't remember anything I know. (*Has down the basket and turns with it in his hands.*) History now—I know a real lot of history. And about birds and things. I'd *like* to talk with her about them. But last week, when I took her to the picnic, I couldn't think out any of 'em to say no more'n a *hen*.

---

[3]Viking Press.

Still onward into adulthood you travel. Nature speaks to you and the answer trembles in your heart, but you can never quite utter it. Then one day you discover Wordsworth's "Lines Written Above Tintern Abbey," and with delight you read them over and over again because he has found both the words and the rhythm to express what has been locked within you:

> ....For I have learned
> To look on nature, not as in the hour
> Of thoughtless youth; but hearing oftentimes
> The still, sad music of humanity,
> Nor harsh nor grating, though of ample power
> To chasten and subdue. And I have felt
> A presence that disturbs me with the joy
> Of elevated thoughts; a sense sublime,
> Of something far more deeply interfused,
> Whose dwelling is the light of setting suns,
> And the round ocean and the living air,
> And the blue sky, and in the mind of man.

When in time your heart bleeds over a wayward child, you come upon David's lament for Absalom in the eighteenth chapter of II Samuel, and you find in that tragic story the picture of suffering parents of all generations, and your own story finds outlet in the heartbroken words of David, "O my son, Absalom, would God I had died for thee, O Absalom, my son, my son!"

You lose a loved one and you seek solitude to walk up and down and ease the aching void in your heart. Then, if never before, the words of Tennyson come welling to your lips with the release of tears to your eyes:

[36]

> And the stately ships go on
> To their haven under the hill,
> But O for the touch of a vanished hand,
> And the sound of a voice that is still.

A war threatens. You find yourself in a dilemma. The voice of the state calls you in one direction, but another voice calls you to a loyalty even higher, a loyalty to mankind as a whole. You are torn between the two. Then you read Sophocles' *Antigone* and discover that 2500 years ago certain Greeks faced a similar dilemma and that Sophocles put your struggle into that great play.

These are but a few familiar instances of the way in which literature provides an expression and an interpretation of your own emotions. Whatever else you may find in it, you will find yourself there.

Second, literature can keep before you the vision of the ideal. It may be the ideal of the perfect state as Matthew Arnold described it in his *Culture and Anarchy*. Or it may be the ideal of a noble character such as Mrs. Charles Kingsley found in her husband. When she wrote his biography she dedicated it thus:

To the Beloved Memory
of
A Righteous Man

Who loved God and Truth above all things.
A man of untarnished honour—
Loyal and chivalrous—gentle and strong—
Modest and humble—tender and true—

[37]

Pitiful to the weak—yearning after the erring—
    Stern to all forms of wrong and oppression
        Yet most stern toward himself—
        Who being angry, yet sinned not.
    Whose highest virtues were known only
To his wife, his children, his servants, and the poor.
    Who lived in the presence of God here,
And passing through the grave and gate of death
    Now liveth unto God for evermore.

F.E.K.

Or it may be the ideal of courage as Plato tells it in his story of Socrates' trial; or J. M. Barrie in his brief description of Captain Scott's last days in the Antarctic. Or it may be the ideal of sacrificial love as Dickens portrays it in the death of Sidney Carton in *The Tale of Two Cities*. Whatever the ideal, it shines in literature as a torch lighting the way for your feet through the darkest of earth's valleys.

Third, literature can give you a better knowledge of human nature. Every great character creation stands for some great trait in human nature. As Mr. Smith pointed out, Ulysses personifies the eternal adventuresomeness of the human spirit. He was the man of resource, self-reliant, fertile in devising escapes from trouble, the "permanent chairman of the Greek ways and means committee." King Arthur personifies the knightly ideals of Christian chivalry; Falstaff, the gross sensualist who denies the very existence of the moral law; Hamlet, the scholar who meditates much but does nothing; Shylock, the victim of race prejudice and persecution; Robinson Crusoe, the man whose world falls apart requiring him to make a fresh start in raw nature. Faust personifies the scholar who fails to find happiness through study and research. David Copperfield personifies the child and youth struggling to understand his elders and to make a place for himself against all the handicaps of poverty and loneliness. And so in more recent literature Babbitt personifies the type of business man who has lost all sense of spiritual values; Mr. Chips, the humble and loyal teacher; George Brush, the irritatingly religious boob who yet wins the respect of modern sophisticates because he has courageously committed himself to a great cause.

Fourth, literature can make the past live for you. Neither Socrates nor Jesus ever left a line of writing. Yet Plato's account of Socrates and the Gospel writers' record of Jesus have made those two great characters more vivid for you than most of the men you meet on the street. You would probably never read any of the military records of the battle of Waterloo, and even if you did you would find them dull going. But read Victor Hugo's *Les Misérables* and you have an unforgettable picture of that struggle in your memory, and the smoke of the battle in your nostrils. You can sit on your own front porch but live in the days when knighthood was in flower if you have in your hand Walter Scott's *Kenilworth* or *Ivanhoe*. Dickens brings a coach and four to your door and invites you to jog along the streets of London and the roads of England of the early nineteenth century with that delightful old ass, Pickwick. In Bernard Shaw's *Saint Joan* you see the maid inspiring an army of French laggards and transforming them into crusaders. And you see also the fifteenth-century reaction as church and state and the Inquisition combine to destroy this troubler. They light the fire under her and you hear the crackle of the flames. Willa Cather in her *O Pioneers* calls the covered wagons of the prairies back from the dust, and you live again with the sturdy farmers who converted a wilderness into fields of golden grain.

Fifth, literature can help you see the glory of the commonplace. The great writers deal with the commonplace—in an uncommonplace way. Shells on the seashore are just shells to most of us. But Oliver Wendell Holmes found "The Chambered Nautilus" in one of them. We have all seen a weary farmer resting on his hoe and probably most of us are familiar with Millet's famous painting, "The Man with a Hoe," but Edwin Markham in his poem on that painting showed us something far more significant than we could have seen without his interpretation. We have all heard larks sing, but the song takes on vastly richer meaning after we have read Shelley's "To a Skylark." Flowers speak a language all their own, but we understand it better when we have read Tennyson's "Flower in a Crannied Wall," and Burns's "To a Mountain Daisy." One secret of Burns's popularity lies in this, that he took the commonplace experiences of the daily life of simple people, penetrated them with his understanding, surrounded them with his affection, and gave them back to the world sparkling with his humor. He was always picking up a piece of coal, holding it high in his poetic hands, and letting the world see that it was essentially a diamond. Before Burns no one seemed to think that the way a poor man spent his Saturday night was of any great consequence, but after he wrote "A Cotter's Saturday Night" everyone realized that it was a cross section of the very heart of the Scottish people.

An oriental water boy may be just a dark skinned machine of low efficiency to the ordinary eye, but read Kipling's "Gunga Din" and ever afterward you will see at least potential loyalty and self-sacrifice in such a servant. And Kipling's rhythm will beat through your mind as at the conclusion of his tale of a battle he describes himself wounded and calling for water:

> " 'Ere's a beggar with a bullet through 'is spleen;
> 'E's chawin' up the ground,
> An' 'e's kickin' all around:
> For Gawd's sake git the water, Gunga Din!"

'E carried me away
To where a *dooli* lay,
An' a bullet come an' drilled the beggar clean.
'E put me safe inside
An' just before 'e died,
"I 'ope you liked your drink," sez Gunga Din.
So I'll meet 'im later on

At the place where 'e is gone—
Where it's always double drill an' no canteen;
'E'll be squattin' on the coals,
Givin' drink to pore damned souls,
An' I'll get a swig in hell from Gunga Din!
    Yes, Din! Din! Din!
  You Lazarushian-leather Gunga Din!
    Though I've belted you an' flayed you,
    By the livin' Gawd that made you,
  You're a better man than I am, Gunga Din!

As I write these lines it is raining. Now rain is
altogether too commonplace a thing in Chicago,
especially in spring after a whole winter of leaden
skies. It irritates me. But under the glass which
covers my desk I see a little poem by Rachel Field.
As I read it my irritation dies away and the patter
of the rain is transformed into soft music.

O lovely rain, fall on the sea,
Silver on silver, liquidly.
Darken each trunk and knotted root,
Give every twig a crystal fruit
To hold, and let the bending grass
Be thick with berries clear as glass. . . .
O lovely, multitudinous rain,
Knock on my door and windowpane;
Stream through the dark, and while I sleep
Your grave and timeless rhythms keep;
Beat like some far, ancestral drum
On this dull brain, this heart grown numb.

That's a bit of what literature can do for you.
The next question is, What books will do it? The
selections that follow have done it for thousands of
others. Many of them are beckoning to you.

ONE HUNDRED INTERESTING BOOKS[4]
Important to the Understanding and Enjoyment of the World Today

(BIOGRAPHIES AND DRAMAS NOT INCLUDED)

The 19th and 20th Centuries

ARNOLD, MATTHEW, 1822-88. *Culture and Anarchy.* A penetrating discussion on the necessity for culture for the salvation and development of democracy.

BARRIE, J. M., 1860——. *Sentimental Tommy.* The tale of a Scotch boy whose literary ambitions were dogged by common human frailty.

BEARD, CHARLES A., 1874——, and MARY R., 1876——. *The Rise of American Civilization.* A simply written yet accurate story of the development of the American nation, stressing social trends rather than political and military events.

BOWERS, CLAUDE, 1879——. *Jefferson and Hamilton.* A dramatic account of the clash of two giants and their conflicting social and political theories.

BRONTE, CHARLOTTE, 1816-55. *Jane Eyre.* The story of an English orphan girl who enters a strange home as governess.

BROWNING, ROBERT, 1812-89. *Poems.* Dramatic lyrics and romances rich in thought and beautiful in form.

BYRON, LORD, 1788-1824. *Poems.* A tortured, sensitive soul expresses his rebellion—and much of ours.

CARLYLE, THOMAS, 1795-1881. *Heroes and Hero Worship.* Critical biographical essays by the Scotch prophet of heroism.

------

[4]There are so many editions of these books that it is desirable to obtain the help of your librarian or bookseller in selecting the edition which best suits your taste or purse. Nearly all of them are now available in editions costing one dollar or less.

CARROLL, LEWIS, 1832-98. *Alice in Wonderland.* This delightfully queer world and its ways through the eyes of a child.

CATHER, WILLA, 1875——. *Death Comes for the Archbishop.* A novel of pioneer days in the American Southwest.

CONRAD, JOSEPH, 1857-1924. *Lord Jim.* The life history of a boy who disgraced himself by an act of cowardice and struggled the rest of his years to regain self-respect.

COOPER, JAMES FENIMORE, 1789-1851. *Leather Stocking Tales.* Stories of American Indians and their conflicts with the first white settlers.

DARWIN, CHARLES, 1809-92. *Origin of Species.* The theory of evolution by natural selection demonstrated by a shipload of evidence. This book divided our scientific era into pre-Darwinian and post-Darwinian.

DICKENS, CHARLES, 1812-70. *David Copperfield, Tale of Two Cities,* and *Great Expectations.* Immortal novels of English poor and middle-class folk.

DOSTOEVSKY, FEODOR, 1822-81. *Crime and Punishment.* Psychological novel about a sensitive man who commits a crime and struggles through the consequences for himself and others. Probably unparalleled in modern fiction in its analysis of the weakness and strength of human souls in the midst of intolerable miseries.

DUMAS, ALEXANDRE, 1802-70. *The Three Musketeers.* Swashbuckling adventures of three soldiers "all for each and each for all" in the days of Louis XIII.

ELIOT, GEORGE, 1819-80. *Romola.* The adventures of an Italian girl in Florence at the height of the Renaissance.

EMERSON, RALPH WALDO, 1803-82. *Essays.* The philosophy of self-reliance by "the wisest American."

GALE, ZONA, 1874——. *Faint Perfume.* Delicate character studies of a sensitive woman, an old man, and a little boy all caught in a domestic tragedy.

GALSWORTHY, JOHN, 1867-1933. *The Forsyte Saga.* An epic of a modern upper middle-class English family and its conflict between love and property.

GARLAND, HAMLIN, 1860-1936. *A Son of the Middle Border.* A realistic novel of the settlement of the Middle West.

HAMSUN, KNUT, 1859——. *The Growth of the Soil.* A Norwegian masterpiece revealing the hardness and the nobility of peasant life.

HARDY, THOMAS, 1840-1928. *The Return of the Native* and *The Mayor of Casterbridge.* Typical Hardy novels of natives of Egdon Heath in dramatic struggles which acquire some of the majestic proportions of Greek tragedy.

HAWTHORNE, NATHANIEL, 1804-64. *The Scarlet Letter.* A moving story of an erring woman in a self-righteous Puritan community in early America.

HILTON, JAMES, 1900——. *Lost Horizon.* The adventure of an Englishman dropped by an airplane from the whirling and confused modern world into a Tibetan Lamasery where he finds the perspective of the centuries. Also *Goodbye Mr. Chips.* The charming tale of an English schoolmaster and how he weaves himself into the affections of his students.

HOWELLS, WILLIAM DEAN, 1837-1920. *The Rise of Silas Lapham.* A quiet novel of a self-made man who comes into conflict with Boston aristocracy.

HUGO, VICTOR, 1802-85. *Les Misérables.* The epic of Jean Valjean and other victims of French social conditions in the era following Napoleon. Often called the world's greatest novel.

JAMES, WILLIAM, 1842-1910. *Varieties of Religious Experience*. A scientific yet sympathetic treatment of the subject by a great psychologist and philosopher.

KEATS, JOHN, 1795-1821. *Poems,* especially odes "To a Nightingale" and "On a Grecian Urn." Unsurpassed in lyric beauty.

KIPLING, RUDYARD, 1865-1936. *The Light That Failed.* A brave man who loves life and action makes his adjustment to blindness.

LAMB, CHARLES, 1775-1834. *Essays of Elia.* Sketches that kept a smile on the face of England in a difficult period.

LANIER, SIDNEY, 1842-81. *Poems,* especially "The Marshes of Glynn" and "Hymns of the Marshes." A Southern poet finds universal significance in local marshes.

LEWIS, SINCLAIR, 1885——. *Arrowsmith.* Realistic novel of an idealistic doctor in conflict with the social evils, especially the commercialism of modern American life. Mr. Lewis was awarded the Nobel Prize for Literature in 1930.

LINCOLN, ABRAHAM, 1809-65. *Addresses.* The inaugurals and the addresses at Gettysburg and Cooper Union are supreme in American political literature.

LINDBERGH, ANNE MORROW, 1907——. *North to the Orient.* The exciting record of the great aviators' flight and the persons and places they met along the way.

LIPPMANN, WALTER, 1889——. *A Preface to Morals.* Keen analysis of changes in moral standards being wrought by science and philosophy.

LONGFELLOW, HENRY WADSWORTH, 1807-92. *Poems,* especially his sonnets and his narrative poem, "Evangeline."

LOWELL, JAMES RUSSELL, 1819-91. *Biglow Papers.* Satirical verse shot through with social passion.

MacMURRAY, JOHN, 1891——. *Creative Society.* A solid little book by an English philosopher who attempts a synthesis of Christianity and Communism.

MACY, JOHN, 1887-1932. *The Story of the World's Literature.* A brilliant and compact survey of great books and the men who made them.

MANSFIELD, KATHERINE, 1889-1923. *The Garden Party.* Charming short stories of English life.

MARX, KARL, 1818-83. *Capital.* An epoch-making book on the economic and social structure of society.

MASEFIELD, JOHN, 1874——. *Selected Poems,* especially "The Story of a Roundhouse," "Cargoes" and "Sea Fever" by England's poet laureate.

MAUGHAM, SOMERSET, 1874——. *Of Human Bondage.* The poignant story of a clubfooted boy, sensitive and rebellious, falling in love with a prostitute and then struggling through to happiness with the aid of stoic philosophy.

MEREDITH, GEORGE, 1828-1909. *The Ordeal of Richard Feverel.* A philosophical novel about a boy who resents the educational system of his father and works out a new one for himself.

MILLAY, EDNA ST. VINCENT, 1892——. *Selected Poems.* Miss Millay is probably the favorite poet of American youth.

"O. HENRY," 1862-1910. *The Four Million.* Short stories of everyday characters in the life of a great city.

PALGRAVE, F. T., 1824-97. *The Golden Treasury.* Classical anthology of verse.

POE, EDGAR ALLEN, 1809-49. *Tales.* Pseudo-scientific mystery and horror stories.

ROBINSON, EDWARD ARLINGTON, 1869-1935. *Collected Poems.* His blank verse narratives are outstanding.

RUSKIN, JOHN, 1819-1900. *Modern Painters.* Essays in art appreciation by the man who is said to have had "the most analytical mind in all Europe" of his day.

SANDBURG, CARL, 1878——. *Selected Poems.* Interpreter of America in verse. Sandburg may yet become our modern Robert Burns.

SCOTT, SIR WALTER, 1771-1832. *Ivanhoe.* Historical novel of the Middle Ages; and *Kenilworth,* of the days when knighthood was in flower.

SHELLEY, PERCY BYSSHE, 1792-1822. *Poems.* Immortal for his "Prometheus Unbound" and "Ode to a Skylark." Singer of man's future freedom, Shelley is often called "the most delicate lyric poet of the 19th century."

SINCLAIR, UPTON, 1878——. *The Brass Check.* An exposé of modern journalism prostituted to commercial ends.

STEVENSON, ROBERT LOUIS, 1850-94. *Dr. Jekyll and Mr. Hyde.* Thrilling story of a dual personality.

TARKINGTON, BOOTH, 1869——. *The Magnificent Ambersons.* The rise and fall of a typical American family during the growth of a Midwest city.

TENNYSON, ALFRED LORD, 1809-92. *Poems.* The prince of lyric poets of the Victorian era.

TOLSTOY, COUNT LEO, 1828-1910. *Anna Karenina.* The great Russian novelist, educator and social reformer here tells the story of a woman who sacrificed everything to love and came into fatal collision with the moral law.

TWAIN, MARK, 1835-1910. *Tom Sawyer* and *Huckleberry Finn.* The perennial adventures of youth against the background of 19th century Missouri.

WELLS, H. G., 1866——. *Outline of History*. A sprightly and often provocative survey of seventy centuries.

WHARTON, EDITH, 1862——. *Ethan Frome*. A bitter New England tragedy by a fine artist.

WHITMAN, WALT, 1819-92. *Leaves of Grass*. To this poet grass is the symbol of democracy and divinity, in both of which he had a passionate trust.

WILDER, THORNTON, 1897——. *The Bridge of San Luis Rey*. Character studies, superbly done, of five persons who met death when the bridge collapsed.

WORDSWORTH, WILLIAM, 1770-1850. *Poems*. Serene and exalting interpretations of nature.

The 16th, 17th, and 18th Centuries

BACON, FRANCIS, 1561-1626. *Essays*. Macaulay said of them, "They have moved the intellects which have moved the world."

BUNYAN, JOHN, 1628-88. *Pilgrim's Progress*. Next to the Bible, probably the most influential book in the religious life of the centuries.

BURNS, ROBERT, 1759-1827. *Poems*. They sing the glories of the commonplace.

CERVANTES, MIGUEL, 1547-1616. *Don Quixote*. The adventures of a knight who had imagination without humor, accompanied by a squire who had humor without imagination. A Spanish satire on the age of chivalry.

DEFOE, DANIEL, 1660-1731. *Robinson Crusoe*. The prototype of all desert island stories.

GIBBON, EDWARD, 1737-94. *Decline and Fall of the Roman Empire*. History made into fascinating literature.

GOLDSMITH, OLIVER, 1728-74. *The Vicar of Wakefield*. The trials of a timid but lovable English clergyman.

HAMILTON, ALEXANDER, 1757-1804. *The Federalist.* Essays which were largely responsible for the ratification of the American Constitution.

JEFFERSON, THOMAS, 1743-1826. *Declaration of Independence.* America's most cherished document.

MILTON, JOHN, 1608-74. *Poems,* especially "Paradise Lost" and "Samson Agonistes." Also *Areopagitica.* A defense of the freedom of the press.

MORE, THOMAS, 1478-1535. *Utopia.* Philosophical essay on the ideal state.

PEPYS, SAMUEL, 1638-1704. *Diary.* Enjoyable for its garrulous gossip and humorous anecdotes and important for its light upon the period.

ROUSSEAU, JEAN JACQUES, 1712-78. *The Social Contract and Other Essays.* These had great influence on the leaders of the American and French revolutions.

SHAKESPEARE, WILLIAM, 1564-1616. *Sonnets.* Superb expressions of human love and pain. (His plays are in the drama list.)

SWIFT, JONATHAN, 1667-1745. *Gulliver's Travels.* A witty allegory satirizing politics, religion and philosophy and questioning man's superiority to animals.

VOLTAIRE, JEAN, 1694-1778. *Candide.* Incisive satire on the idea that "all is for the best in this best of all possible worlds."

Medieval and Ancient

ABELARD, 1079-1142. Letters of *Heloise and Abelard.* One of the great love stories of the Middle Ages —and a true one.

ARABIAN NIGHTS. A glorious collection of stories of myth and magic from oriental lore. Aladdin, Sinbad, and Ali Baba are household terms in every land.

ARISTOTLE, 384-322 B. C. *Ethics*. The great pupil of Plato and "master of those who know" here expounds his doctrine that happiness is obtained through moderation in all things. Also *Poetics*. Valuable for its compact and sure analysis of the laws of drama.

AUGUSTINE, 354-430. *Confessions* and *City of God*. In the midst of the breakup of the Roman empire this great scholar and philosopher dreamed of a new social order.

BIBLE. The history, poetry, and expanding philosophy of man's quest for God among the Hebrews and early Christians. The foundational book of Christian civilization.

CAESAR, CAIUS JULIUS, 100-44 B. C. *Commentaries*. "Crystal-clear reports on the techniques of successful military campaigns."

CHAUCER, GEOFFREY, 1340-1400. *The Canterbury Tales*. Dramatic stories in verse portraying English people and customs of the Middle Ages.

CICERO, 106-43 B. C. *Essays* and *Orations*. Mature wisdom on old age, friendship and politics by the greatest of Latin orators.

DANTE, 1265-1321. *The Divine Comedy*. A poetic allegory of the whole life and destiny of man in time and in eternity.

EPICTETUS, 50-125. *Golden Sayings*. A slave who became the famous teacher of stoicism sets forth shrewd and practical maxims for daily life.

HOMER, before 850 B. C. *The Iliad* and *The Odyssey*. Epic stories of the Trojan War and of Ulysses told so vividly that they are still more alive than most modern adventure stories.

PLATO, 429-348 B. C. *The Dialogues*. In "The Apology" and "The Crito" we are given dramatic accounts of the trial and death of Socrates. In "The

[51]

Republic" the philosopher blueprints the ideal state, its justice and the relation of the individual to it.

St. Francis of Assisi, 1182-1226. *Little Flowers of St. Francis* and *The Mirror of Perfection.* Although St. Francis did not write these, he is their central character. They are charming sketches of the first Brothers of the Franciscan Order in Medieval Italy.

THE CURTAIN RISES

WHAT is drama? Drama is the art of creating characters who in two hours make us laugh and cry and sit anxiously upon the edges of our seats awaiting the outcome of their struggles. Percival Wilde gives a more formal and probably more accurate definition. "A drama," he says, "is an orderly representation of life arousing emotion in an audience." Aristotle went deeper yet. The function of tragedy, he tells us is "to purge the passions of pity and fear by an exalted use thereof." Just what did he mean by that? When you go into a theater your mind is apt to be centered upon yourself. You have fears for yourself, pity for yourself. But soon after the play begins you forget yourself and transfer your fear and pity to some character upon the stage with whose destiny your emotions become involved. That transference of fear and pity from yourself to someone else is an exalting and cleansing experience.

To accomplish this emotional effect the dramatist has a technique which he has been working out and adapting and modifying for twenty-five hundred years, or ever since the days of Aeschylus and Aristophanes. In general that technique consists (1) in creating a central character who has life and passion and who knows what he wants; (2) in thrusting that character into some conflict common to the experience or observation of the audience; (3) in confronting him with choices which must be made and out of which the actions of the other characters flow; (4) in bringing the conflict to a sharp crisis under the pressure of which the central character is broken open and his soul revealed.

When the dramatist stands on the edge of his central character's personality and looks down into the crater of that soul and sees him as a creature of the moment, something to smile at and pass on, the play is usually a comedy. When the dramatist views his character from the standpoint of eternity, however, and sees him as infinitely small and yet infinitely significant, the play is apt to be a tragedy.

The difference between a drama and a novel lies chiefly in the fact that the novelist shows the *development* of a character through a considerable period of time, whereas the dramatist shows little or no development but *reveals a character in some high moment of crisis*. Take Willa Cather's *O Pioneers* as an example of a novel. At the beginning of the book she describes a great middle western farm and a little girl upon it. The farm is very, very large, and the girl very, very small. In fact the girl is only one of the many bits of life on that vast acreage. As she grows up and inherits the farm from her pioneer father, she has to meet and struggle with the forces of nature—drouth, flood, insect pests, wind and hail, snow and blistering sun. She meets her problems as they come; wins out over some; is defeated by others. All the time she grows bigger, not only in stature but in the dimensions of her soul. By the time you reach the last chapter you see that soul grown to heroic proportions and the vast farm is located somewhere in one corner of her heart. That is the sort of thing every good novelist tries to do.

Take Maxwell Anderson's *Valley Forge* as an example of drama. You meet George Washington not as a boy at the beginning of his life, but as a revolutionary general at the crisis of his career. In that crisis he is confronted on the one hand by a British army of superior numbers, on the other by a group of hucksters in Congress who have lost all enthusiasm for the war since any trade advantage they might have won from it is gone. Against these two powerful enemies Washington must struggle. His own army is a rag-tag, and bobtail affair, a motley collection of farmers, starved, half naked, and short of ammunition. But those farmers have within them a passion for freedom. They are willing to die for it and they trust Washington to lead them. Mr. Anderson's drama presents scenes from only five days of this struggle. We see Washington beaten and ready to give up, convinced that it is useless to fight on. "I have given myself to a footless insurrection, drained out my blood on a mock heroic altar, made a monk of what might have been a man. And I will get for that what Jack Cade got: three lines in a history, touching a minor figure in a brief uprising that died down early in some year of our Lord." But his men rally round him. In a foray two or three of those he loved best are killed. The spirit and sacrifice of his men put new heart in Washington. He turns to General Howe, who has come to receive his surrender, and announces that there will be no surrender.

> ....The spirit of earth
> moves over earth like flame and finds fresh home
> when the old's burned out. It stands over this my
>   country
> in this dark year, and stands like a pillar of fire
> to show us an uncouth clan, unread, harsh-spoken,
> but followers of dream, a dream that men
> shall bear no burdens save of their own choosing,
> shall walk upright, masterless, doff a hat to none,
> and choose their gods! It's destined to win, this
>   dream,
> weak though we are. Even if we should fail,
> it's destined to win!

Thus the dramatist shows us a great soul in crisis, revealing its weakness and strength, and when the curtain falls upon the last act, we know that we have been standing before one of the men "who lift the age they inhabit—till all men walk on higher ground in that lifetime." That's the sort of thing every good dramatist tries to do.

When you read a drama, therefore, you look for a different kind of enjoyment than you find in a novel. Apply to a drama these five tests; if it passes them you will be coming back to it time and again and looking forward to seeing it acted:

1. Does it move you to laughter or tears, or both?

2. Does it create for you some character worth knowing or remembering, someone you would like to talk to? Does that character know what he wants? Does he have to make important choices—as, for example, Hamlet's "To be, or not to be," or Washington's to surrender or to carry on?

3. Is that character in the midst of some conflict that involves you, or might some day involve you?

4. Does that conflict rise to a climax and keep you in suspense until you know the outcome?

5. When the final curtain falls do you find that you have forgotten yourself for two hours and now return to your own skin refreshed and happier within?

If the play meets those tests, salute the playwright. He has done his job well. If it doesn't, try another.

FIFTY DRAMAS
Which Have Made People Laugh and Cry—and Think

The 19th and 20th Centuries

ANDERSON, MAXWELL, 1888——. *Both Your Houses.* What happened to a political reformer in Congress. *Valley Forge.* George Washington against the British army, the hucksters in Congress, conniving subordinates, a designing woman, a tough winter, and other enemies. *Winterset.* Legal justice miscarries and half a dozen lives spend years in torment.

ATLAS, LEOPOLD, 1907——. *Wednesday's Child.* What divorce does to the children in a modern home.

BARRIE, SIR JAMES, 1860——. *Dear Brutus.* Each member of an English company is given a second chance at making an important life decision. *What Every Woman Knows.* A plain Scotch girl discovers that man was made from Adam's funnybone instead of his rib as commonly supposed.

BARRY, PHILIP, 1896——. *Tomorrow and Tomorrow.* The old triangle with a new interpretation. *You and I.* The conflict between the inner urge to do the creative thing and the outer constraint to make a living for one's family.

CAPEK, KAREL, 1890——. *R. U. R.* An allegory of modern man conquered by his machines.

CHEKHOV, ANTON, 1860-1904. *The Cherry Orchard.* The old order of luxury in a Russian family gives place to a new one of poverty.

CONNELLY, MARC, 1890——. *The Green Pastures.* The Bible as it filters through the imagination of Negroes.

CROTHERS, RACHEL, 1878——. *When Ladies Meet.* Two women in a modern triangle discover each other's viewpoints and together renounce the philandering male.

FERBER, EDNA, 1888——. *Minick*. A lovable but devastating father-in-law comes to live with a young married couple and nearly ruins everything.

FERRIS, WALTER, 1882——. *Death Takes a Holiday*. (Translated and revised from the Italian of Casella.) Death takes on human flesh and comes on a holiday to earth where he learns why some fear him and others look upon him as a Portal of Hope.

FLAVIN, MARTIN, 1883——. *Amaco*. A bitter story of modern business and its effect on human souls.

GALE, ZONA, 1874——. *Miss Lulu Bett*. The tender and humorous romance of a household drudge.

GALSWORTHY, JOHN, 1867-1933. *Strife*. An episode in the perennial struggle between capital and labor. *Loyalties*. A study of the conflicting loyalties to class and race and profession when not subordinated to any higher loyalty.

GREEN, PAUL, 1894——. *In Abraham's Bosom*. The story of a Southern Negro striving valiantly for cultural advancement against the inertia of his people and the prejudice of the whites.

GREGORY, LADY, 1859-1932. *Seven Short Plays*. Charming stories of Irish folk.

HOWARD, SIDNEY, 1891——. *The Silver Cord*. A mother love which becomes perverted and nearly destroys two sons and their sweethearts. Also *Alien Corn*. An Italian musician and his daughter in the midst of the repressions of a Midwest college town.

IBSEN, HENRIK, 1828-1906. *The Doll's House* and *Ghosts*. Ibsen, the father of modern drama, is concerned not only with stories but with ideas; not only with what people do but with why they do it—especially with their subconscious motives. These two plays are typical of the twenty-eight he wrote.

LEVY, BENN, 1900——. *The Devil Passes.* The devil in the garb of a vicar comes to an English parish and does the work of the Lord in making individuals choose the values by which they will live.

MAETERLINCK, MAURICE, 1862-1936. *The Bluebird.* A fantasy of peasant life together with glimpses into the lands of Memory, of Happiness, and of Unborn Children.

MILNE, A. A., 1882——. *Mr. Pim Passes By.* The failing memory of a delightful old gentleman wreaks havoc in an English country home.

NICHOLS, ROBERT, 1893——, and BROWNE, MAURICE, 1891——. *Wings Over Europe.* A young artist-scientist discovers a way to harness the energy of the atom and then calls upon the British Cabinet to reorganize human society on a peace basis.

O'NEILL, EUGENE, 1888——. *The Hairy Ape.* An inarticulate stoker tries to rise in the scale of life and to find the place in life where he belongs. *Mourning Becomes Electra.* The classic Greek story retold with modern characters. *Days Without End.* The tale of an adultery, its punishment and ultimate forgiveness. (Mr. O'Neill was awarded the Nobel Prize for Literature in 1936.)

ROBINSON, LENNOX, 1886——. *The White Headed Boy.* The favorite son of an Irish mother brings trouble to the rest of the family and escapes the consequences.

ROSTAND, EDMOND, 1868-1918. *Cyrano de Bergerac.* A homely knight fights for his honor and his love. One of the greatest dramas of all time.

SHAW, GEORGE BERNARD, 1856——. *Candida.* The wife of a successful clergyman has to choose between him and a young poet who loves her. *Saint Joan.* The story of the immortal maid done into strong drama without sacrifice of historical accuracy.

[60]

TOLSTOY, COUNT LEO, 1828-1910. *The Redemption.*
A sensitive Russian plumbs the lower depths of
despair and finds ultimate redemption in sacrifice.

The 16th, 17th, and 18th Centuries

GOETHE, JOHANN WOLFGANG, 1749-1842. *Faust.* The
life experience of Goethe and the spiritual history of mankind dramatized.

MARLOWE, CHRISTOPHER, 1564-93. *Dr. Faustus.* The old
story of the weary scholar who sold his soul to the
devil in exchange for youth and beauty and love.

SCHILLER, JOHANN I. F., 1759-1805. *Wilhelm Tell.*
A poetic play of the struggle for political
freedom.

SHAKESPEARE, WILLIAM, 1564-1616. *Romeo and Juliet,
Hamlet, Othello, King Lear, Macbeth.* These are
but five of the thirty-nine plays of the greatest of
English playwrights. The rest are omitted only
because this entire list is limited to fifty.

Ancient

AESCHYLUS, 525-456 B. C. *Agamemnon, The Libation-
Bearers, Eumenides, Prometheus Bound.* The first
three revolve around the story of Orestes who
murdered his mother because she had slain his
father. His sin is finally expiated after much
struggle and suffering among both gods and men.
The fourth is the drama of a man who defied
the gods in his determination to serve his fellow
men. All of these plays are in heroic verse. They
have a nobility and majesty rarely if ever
equaled.

ARISTOPHANES, 445-385 B. C. *The Frogs.* Satirical comedy on the Greek tragedians. *The Clouds.*
A lyrical burlesque poking fun at Socrates.

EURIPIDES, 480-406 B. C. *Medea.* A jealous woman
slays her rival and her own children as a revenge

upon their father. Brutal enough, but the playwright's treatment lifts it to high tragedy.

JOB. By an unknown author, a contemporary of Aeschylus and Sophocles. A Hebrew philosophical drama on the problem of human suffering.

SOPHOCLES, 496-406 B. C. *Antigone.* The story of a Greek girl who faced a choice between loyalty to the state and loyalty to the gods when the two loyalties came into conflict—and paid the price. *King Oedipus.* The tragedy of a young hero who saved his city, then unwittingly married his mother and later suffered blindness and exile in consequence.

POSTSCRIPT

YOUR library can supply you with the books recommended by Dr. Eastman. Most libraries also can offer you individualized advice in selecting the editions which will best meet your taste. And when your reading opens up new channels your librarian will gladly help you plot your course. Your bookseller, of course, will be glad to provide you with the editions which suit your purse.